M000097251

My Lenten Journey 2019

Daily Challenges, Questions, & Quotes to Guide You Through the Holy Season of Lent

By Travis and Jennifer Rainey

Copyright © 2019
All rights reserved.
ISBN: 9781796467611
Scripture taken from the Catholic Edition of the
Revised Standard Version of the Bible,
copyright © 1965, 1966
National Council of the Churches
of Christ in the United States of America.
Used by permission.
All rights reserved worldwide.

This book is dedicated to our third child, Richard.
We love you, sweetheart.

Lent is a special time when we should grow closer to the Lord.

This book will guide you through each day of Lent with:
- Quotes from Saints
- Questions that make you think about your faith
- Challenges that encourage prayer, good deeds, and further reflection
- Space to write prayer requests and what you are thankful for
- Selected feast days
- Days of abstinence marked ☓

We hope this book helps you through the holy journey of Lent.

Jennifer and Travis Rainey
February 2019

Lenten Goals

Here are a few ideas for your Lenten resolutions. You could choose one or more of these ideas or come up with your own.

- Make the Morning Offering (page 56) daily.
- Make the Stations of the Cross at your church.
- Pray the Holy Rosary daily.
- Concentrate on one or more of the Acts of Mercy.
- Try to eliminate a particular sin or vice.
- Limit television or social media.
- Pray the Divine Mercy Chaplet (page 64).
- Pray the Seven Sorrows Chaplet (page 67).
- Go to Mass more than once each week.
- Read the Holy Scriptures daily.
- Read a spiritual book.
- Start First Friday or First Saturday devotions.
- Treat loved ones with extra love, concern, service, and generosity.

My Lenten Goals

Wednesday, March 6, 2019 ✝

Ash Wednesday (Day of Fasting and Abstinence)

"Fasting cleanses the soul... renders the heart contrite and humble, scatters the clouds of concupiscence, quenches the fire of lust, kindles the true light of chastity." ~ St. Augustine

How can I, with God's help, resist temptations this Lent?

_____

_____

_____

_____

_____

I am praying for:

- _____   - _____

I am thankful for:

- _____   - _____

Today's Challenge: Pray the Rosary, asking to grow closer to God during this Lenten journey.

Thursday, March 7, 2019

Sts. Perpetua and Felicity

"(I cannot) call myself any other than I am, that is to say, a Christian." ~ St. Perpetua (when facing martyrdom for her faith)

How would I respond if faced with martyrdom?

_____

_____

_____

_____

_____

I am praying for:

- _____   - _____

I am thankful for:

- _____   - _____

Today's Challenge: Pray for people who are being martyred around the world.

Friday, March 8, 2019 ⊂×

St. John of God

"Any misfortune of yours affects me too, and I rejoice over all your blessings." ~ *St. John of God*

How can I empathize more with people I know?

_____

_____

_____

_____

_____

I am praying for:

- _____   - _____

I am thankful for:

- _____   - _____

Today's Challenge: Call a family member, maybe one who is homebound, and listen carefully to their joys and sorrows.

Saturday, March 9, 2019

"Great holiness consists in carrying out the 'little duties' of each moment." ~ Saint Josemaría Escrivá

What "little duties" could I do for Jesus today?

_____

_____

_____

_____

_____

I am praying for:

- _____   - _____

I am thankful for:

- _____   - _____

Today's Challenge: Pray the Morning Offering (page 56).

Sunday, March 10, 2019
First Sunday of Lent

"The Eucharist bathes the tormented soul in light and love. Then the soul appreciates these words, 'Come all you who are sick, I will restore your health.' " ~ St. Bernadette

How has the Eucharist transformed my life?

_____

_____

_____

_____

_____

I am praying for:

- _____   - _____

I am thankful for:

- _____   - _____

Today's Challenge: Spend some time this week in Eucharistic Adoration or in meditation on the Holy Eucharist.

Monday, March 11, 2019

"By the anxieties and worries of this life Satan tries to dull man's heart and make a dwelling for himself there."

~ Saint Francis of Assisi

Why do I worry? How can I better trust God?

_____

_____

_____

_____

_____

I am praying for:

\- _____   \- _____

I am thankful for:

\- _____   \- _____

Today's Challenge: Read Matthew 6:25-34.

Tuesday, March 12, 2019

"You don't climb a mountain in leaps and bounds, but by taking it slowly." ~ *Pope St. Gregory the Great*

How can I be more patient with God's plan for me?

_____

_____

_____

_____

_____

I am praying for:

- _____   - _____

I am thankful for:

- _____   - _____

Today's Challenge: Evaluate your expectations for Lent. Are they reasonable?

Wednesday, March 13, 2019

"Nobody can fight properly and boldly for the faith if he clings to a fear of being stripped of earthly possessions."

~ St. Peter Damian

How can I become less attached to my possessions?

_____

_____

_____

_____

_____

I am praying for:

- _____   - _____

I am thankful for:

- _____   - _____

Today's Challenge: Look around at your belongings and see if there is anything you could give away, donate, or sell.

Thursday, March 14, 2019

"The most powerful weapon to conquer the devil is humility. For, as he does not know at all how to employ it, neither does he know how to defend himself from it." ~ Saint Vincent de Paul

In what areas should I work on my humility?

_____

_____

_____

_____

_____

I am praying for:

- _____   - _____

I am thankful for:

- _____   - _____

Today's Challenge: Pray the Litany of Humility (page 68).

Friday, March 15, 2019 ∝

"Love Christ and put nothing before His Love. He is joy,
He is life, He is light. Christ is Everything."
~ St. Porphyrius

Do I put anything above God? How can I change?

_____

_____

_____

_____

_____

I am praying for:

\- _____   \- _____

I am thankful for:

\- _____   \- _____

Today's Challenge: Pray the Divine Praises (page 55).

Saturday, March 16, 2019

"You can win more converts with a spoonful of honey than with a barrelful of vinegar." ~ St. Francis de Sales

How can I project more joy to others?

_____

_____

_____

_____

_____

I am praying for:

-   _____   -   _____

I am thankful for:

-   _____   -   _____

Today's Challenge: Think about someone close to you who irritates you and then try to do a kind deed for that person.

Sunday, March 17, 2019

Second Sunday of Lent

"Christ with me, Christ before me, Christ behind me, Christ in me, Christ beneath me, Christ above me, Christ on my right, Christ on my left, Christ where I lie, Christ where I sit, Christ where I arise..." ~ St. Patrick

How can I place Jesus in the center of my life?

_____

_____

_____

_____

_____

I am praying for:

- _____   - _____

I am thankful for:

- _____   - _____

Today's Challenge: Pray for priests who, like St. Patrick, are far from their native homes.

Monday, March 18, 2019
St. Cyril of Jerusalem

"Your accumulated offenses do not surpass the multitude of God's mercies: your wounds do not surpass the great Physician's skill." ~ St. Cyril of Jerusalem

Do I trust that God will forgive all of my sins?

_____

_____

_____

_____

_____

I am praying for:

- _____   - _____

I am thankful for:

- _____   - _____

Today's Challenge: Make an examination of conscience today and plan to go to Confession soon.

Tuesday, March 19, 2019

St. Joseph, Spouse of the Blessed Virgin Mary

"The Lord has arrayed Joseph, like with a sun, in all which the saints possess together in regard to light and splendor." ~ *St. Gregory of Nazianzus*

How can I imitate St. Joseph's obedience and faith?

_____

_____

_____

_____

_____

I am praying for:

- _____   - _____

I am thankful for:

- _____   - _____

Today's Challenge: Ask St. Joseph to intercede for all families.

Wednesday, March 20, 2019

"Just take everything exactly as it is, put it in God's hands, and leave it with Him. Then you will be able to rest in him — really rest." ~ St. Edith Stein

How do I view God as my "Abba," my father?

_____

_____

_____

_____

_____

I am praying for:

- _____   - _____

I am thankful for:

- _____   - _____

Today's Challenge: In all of your tasks today, start with a prayer that God will guide your actions.

Thursday, March 21, 2019

"Joy is a net of love by which we catch souls."
~ St. Teresa of Calcutta

How can I live a more joyful life, even during trials?

_____

_____

_____

_____

_____

I am praying for:

- _____   - _____

I am thankful for:

- _____   - _____

Today's Challenge: List several of your blessings, and thank God for each one.

Friday, March 22, 2019 ⳩

"Loving God, loving people, is my whole life; may it always be my whole life, this is what I hope for."
~ Blessed Charles de Foucauld

What are my top three priorities in life?

_____

_____

_____

_____

_____

I am praying for:

- _____   - _____

I am thankful for:

- _____   - _____

Today's Challenge: Spend your day putting other people ahead of yourself, especially in little ways.

Saturday, March 23, 2019

"The wider our contemplation of creation, the grander is our conception of God." ~ *St. Cyril of Jerusalem*

Do I see God's Hand in Creation? Do I thank Him?

_____

_____

_____

_____

_____

I am praying for:

\-   _____   \-   _____

I am thankful for:

\-   _____   \-   _____

Today's Challenge: Read Psalm 19:1-6.

Sunday, March 24, 2019
Third Sunday of Lent

"Receive the Body and Blood of Christ very frequently. The sight of a Christian's lips red with the Blood of Christ terrifies the enemy." ~ St. Peter Damian

Do I appreciate the gift of Jesus' Body and Blood?

_____

_____

_____

_____

_____

I am praying for:

- _____   - _____

I am thankful for:

- _____   - _____

Today's Challenge: Try to arrive at Mass early today, so that you will have time to pray and prepare for this Sacrament.

Monday, March 25, 2019
The Annunciation of the Lord

"Our Lady listens attentively to what God wants, ponders what she doesn't fully understand and asks about what she doesn't know. Then she gives herself completely to doing God's Will." ~ St. Josemaria Escriva

How can I say "yes" to God today?

_____

_____

_____

_____

_____

I am praying for:

- _____   - _____

I am thankful for:

- _____   - _____

Today's Challenge: Read Luke 1:26-38 and pray the Joyful Mysteries of the Rosary.

Tuesday, March 26, 2019

"If there be a true way that leads to the Everlasting Kingdom, it is most certainly that of suffering, patiently endured." ~ *Saint Colette*

How can I patiently endure my trials today?

_____
_____
_____
_____
_____

I am praying for:

- _____   - _____

I am thankful for:

- _____   - _____

Today's Challenge: When something unpleasant happens, offer it up for the Holy Souls in Purgatory.

Wednesday, March 27, 2019

"Truly, matters in the world are in a bad state; but if you and I begin in earnest to reform ourselves, a really good beginning will have been made." ~ St. Peter of Alcantara

Do I notice imperfections in others more than myself?

_____
_____
_____
_____
_____

I am praying for:

- _____   - _____

I am thankful for:

- _____   - _____

Today's Challenge: Pray for society, that people will have a strong Christian faith that radiates kindness and goodness.

Thursday, March 28, 2019

"The first end I propose in our daily work is to do the Will of God; secondly, to do it in the manner He wills it; and thirdly to do it because it is His Will."

~ St. Elizabeth Ann Seton

How can I spend my time wisely today?

_____

_____

_____

_____

_____

I am praying for:

- _____   - _____

I am thankful for:

- _____   - _____

Today's Challenge: Pray that God makes His Will obvious to you and that you have the courage to follow it.

Friday, March 29, 2019 ✕

"You do not need to wallow in guilt. Wallow in the mercy of God." ~ St. John Vianney

How have I allowed past sins to affect my life now?

_____

_____

_____

_____

_____

I am praying for:

-   _____   -   _____

I am thankful for:

-   _____   -   _____

Today's Challenge: Make the Act of Contrition (page 57).

Saturday, March 30, 2019

"We must either command (our passions) or be enslaved by them."
~ St. Dominic

How can I fight my most common sins?

_____

_____

_____

_____

_____

I am praying for:

- _____   - _____

I am thankful for:

- _____   - _____

Today's Challenge: If you have broken your Lenten resolution, start again today.

Sunday, March 31, 2019
Fourth Sunday of Lent

"Every Christian must be a living book in which others can read the teaching of the Gospel."
~ St. Joseph of Leonissa

By my deeds and words, is it obvious I'm a Christian?

_____

_____

_____

_____

_____

I am praying for:

- _____   - _____

I am thankful for:

- _____   - _____

Today's Challenge: Read one or two chapters of the Gospel of John.

Monday, April 1, 2019

"Speak ill of no one and avoid the company of those who talk about their neighbors." ~ *St. Jacinta Marto of Fátima*

Do I gossip about others? How can I stop?

_____

_____

_____

_____

_____

I am praying for:

-   _____   -   _____

I am thankful for:

-   _____   -   _____

Today's Challenge: If you gossip, try to go a week without talking about others. Pray for those you have gossiped about in the past.

Tuesday, April 2, 2019
St. Francis of Paola

"Pardon one another so that later on you will not remember the injury. The recollection of an injury… is a rusty arrow and poison for the soul. It puts all virtue to flight." ~ St. Francis of Paola

Who do I have a difficult time forgiving? Why?

_____

_____

_____

_____

_____

I am praying for:

- _____   - _____

I am thankful for:

- _____   - _____

Today's Challenge: Make a resolution to forgive someone who has wronged you in the past.

Wednesday, April 3, 2019
St. Richard of Chichester

"I wish not merely to be called Christian, but also to be Christian." ~ St. Ignatius of Antioch

What does it mean to "be Christian"?

_____

_____

_____

_____

_____

I am praying for:

- _____   - _____

I am thankful for:

- _____   - _____

Today's Challenge: Read the Bible each day between now and Easter.

Thursday, April 4, 2019
St. Isidore of Seville

"Confession heals, Confession justifies, Confession grants pardon of sin…. In Confession there is a chance for mercy. Believe it firmly. Hope and have confidence in Confession."
~ St. Isidore of Seville

How has Confession affected my life?

_____

_____

_____

_____

_____

I am praying for:

- _____   - _____

I am thankful for:

- _____   - _____

Today's Challenge: If you haven't been to Confession this Lent, make plans to go before Easter.

Friday, April 5, 2019 ✦
First Friday

"When you approach the tabernacle, remember that He has been waiting for you for twenty centuries."
~ St. Josemaria Escriva

How can I thank our Eucharistic King?

_____

_____

_____

_____

_____

I am praying for:

- _____   - _____

I am thankful for:

- _____   - _____

Today's Challenge: If you are able, attend Mass or Eucharistic Adoration today. Otherwise, read the Gospel of John chapter 6.

Saturday, April 6, 2019
First Saturday

"Act as if every day were the last of your life, and each action the last you perform."

~ St. Alphonsus Maria de Liguori

What would I do if I knew I would die tomorrow?

_____

_____

_____

_____

_____

I am praying for:

-   _____   -   _____

I am thankful for:

-   _____   -   _____

Today's Challenge: Pray the Divine Mercy Chaplet (page 64).

Sunday, April 7, 2019
Fifth Sunday of Lent

"Heaven for me is hidden in a little Host Where Jesus, my Spouse, is veiled for love."
~ St. Therese of Lisieux

Do my actions show my belief in the Real Presence?

_____

_____

_____

_____

_____

I am praying for:

- _____   - _____

I am thankful for:

- _____   - _____

Today's Challenge: When you attend Mass, be especially reverent, and it will serve as a witness to others.

Monday, April 8, 2019

"Maintain a spirit of peace and you will save a thousand souls." ~ Saint Seraphim of Sarov

How can I be peaceful even during trials?

_____

_____

_____

_____

_____

I am praying for:

- _____   - _____

I am thankful for:

- _____   - _____

Today's Challenge: Try to maintain your inner peace all day. If you start to become angry or anxious, pray for God's peace.

Tuesday, April 9, 2019

"May all Christians be found worthy of either the pure white crown of a holy life or the royal red crown of martyrdom." ~ St. Cyprian

Am I prepared to die a martyr for the faith?

_____

_____

_____

_____

_____

I am praying for:

- _____   - _____

I am thankful for:

- _____   - _____

Today's Challenge: Read about the lives of two or three martyrs.

Wednesday, April 10, 2019

"Let nothing disturb you, nothing frighten you; all things are passing; God never changes."
~ Saint Teresa of Avila

Do I trust my future to God?

_____

_____

_____

_____

_____

I am praying for:

-   _____   -   _____

I am thankful for:

-   _____   -   _____

Today's Challenge: Pray for God to work through you, even with all of your weaknesses and imperfections.

Thursday, April 11, 2019
St. Stanislaus

"The gate of Heaven is very low; only the humble can enter it." ~ St. Elizabeth Ann Seton

Am I willing to "decrease" like John the Baptist?

_____

_____

_____

_____

_____

I am praying for:

- _____   - _____

I am thankful for:

- _____   - _____

Today's Challenge: Pray the Litany of Humility (page 68).

Friday, April 12, 2019 ⳇ

"Therefore, do not be anxious about tomorrow, for tomorrow will be anxious for itself. Let the day's own trouble be sufficient for the day." ~ Matthew 6:34

How can I live in the moment and worry less?

_____

_____

_____

_____

_____

I am praying for:

- _____   - _____

I am thankful for:

- _____   - _____

Today's Challenge: Read the Promises of the Sacred Heart (pages 62-63).

Saturday, April 13, 2019

"The most holy Passion of Jesus Christ is the most efficacious means to convert obstinate sinners."
~ St. Paul of Cross

How often do I pray for those who have hurt me?

_____
_____
_____
_____
_____

I am praying for:

-   _____   -   _____

I am thankful for:

-   _____   -   _____

Today's Challenge: Look at a Crucifix, meditating on Jesus' Love for everyone, including sinners.

Sunday, April 14, 2019
Palm Sunday of the Passion of the Lord

"The remembrance of the most holy Passion of Jesus Christ is the door through which the soul enters into intimate union with God, interior recollection, and most sublime contemplation." ~ St. Paul of the Cross

What does Jesus' Passion mean to me?

_____

_____

_____

_____

_____

I am praying for:

- _____   - _____

I am thankful for:

- _____   - _____

Today's Challenge: Pray the Rosary today, with the intention of having a fruitful Holy Week.

Monday, April 15, 2019

"While the world changes, the cross stands firm."
~ Saint Bruno

As society grows more sinful, do I still trust God?

_____

_____

_____

_____

_____

I am praying for:

- _____   - _____

I am thankful for:

- _____   - _____

Today's Challenge: Pray that more people will come to know the love of Jesus.

Tuesday, April 16, 2019

"Why must we suffer? Because here below pure Love
cannot exist without suffering. O Jesus, Jesus, I no longer
feel my cross when I think of yours."
~ St. Bernadette Soubirous

How can I lighten the suffering of other people?

_____

_____

_____

_____

_____

I am praying for:

-   _____   -   _____

I am thankful for:

-   _____   -   _____

Today's Challenge: Do something to help someone
today – a friend, co-worker, or stranger.

Wednesday, April 17, 2019

"Apart from the cross, there is no other ladder by which we may get to Heaven."
~ St. Rose of Lima

How can I unite my own suffering to Jesus' suffering?

_____

_____

_____

_____

_____

I am praying for:

- _____   - _____

I am thankful for:

- _____   - _____

Today's Challenge: Pray the Seven Sorrows Chaplet (page 67).

Thursday, April 18, 2019
Holy Thursday

"When you look at the Crucifix, you understand how much Jesus loved you then. When you look at the Sacred Host, you understand how much Jesus loves you now."
~ St. Teresa of Calcutta

How could I describe the Eucharist to a nonbeliever?

_____

_____

_____

_____

_____

I am praying for:

- _____   - _____

I am thankful for:

- _____   - _____

Today's Challenge: Attend Mass if you are able, and pray the Luminous Mysteries of the Rosary.

Friday, April 19, 2019 ⚲

Good Friday (Day of Fasting and Abstinence)

"There is no practice more profitable for the entire sanctification of the soul than the frequent meditation of the sufferings of Jesus Christ."
~ Saint Alphonsus de Liguori

How can I thank Jesus for dying for our sins?

_____
_____
_____
_____
_____

I am praying for:

- _____   - _____

I am thankful for:

- _____   - _____

Today's Challenge: Attend a Good Friday service if you are able, and start the Divine Mercy Novena.

Saturday, April 20, 2019
Holy Saturday

"Mount Calvary is the academy of love."

~ St. Francis de Sales

How can I show God's Love to others?

_____

_____

_____

_____

_____

I am praying for:

- _____   - _____

I am thankful for:

- _____   - _____

Today's Challenge: Pray for the Candidates and Catechumens who will enter the Catholic Church tonight.

Sunday, April 21, 2019
Easter Sunday of the Resurrection of Our Lord

"We are the Easter People and Alleluia is our song!"
~ St. John Paul II

How can I continue growing in my faith after Easter?

_____
_____
_____
_____
_____

I am praying for:

- _____   - _____

I am thankful for:

- _____   - _____

Today's Challenge: Try to keep one of your new
devotions or prayers throughout the year.

Catholic Prayers

The Prayer by William-Adolphe Bouguereau

The Our Father

Our Father who art in Heaven, hallowed be Thy name; Thy Kingdom come; Thy will be done on earth as it is in Heaven. Give us this day our daily bread; and forgive us our trespasses as we forgive those who trespass against us; and lead us not into temptation, but deliver us from evil. Amen.

The Hail Mary

Hail Mary, full of grace! The Lord is with thee; blessed art thou among women, and blessed is the fruit of thy womb, Jesus. Holy Mary, Mother of God, pray for us sinners, now and at the hour of our death. Amen.

The Glory Be

Glory be to the Father, and to the Son, and to the Holy Spirit. As it was in the beginning, is now, and ever shall be, world without end. Amen.

The Fátima Prayer

O my Jesus, forgive us our sins, save us from the fires of hell, and lead all souls to Heaven, especially those most in need of Thy mercy. Amen.

Grace Before Meals

Bless us, O Lord, and these Thy gifts, which we are about to receive from Thy bounty, through Christ our Lord. Amen.

Grace After Meals

We give Thee thanks for all your benefits, O Almighty God, Who lives and reigns forever; and may the souls of the faithful departed, through the mercy of God, rest in peace. Amen.

Hail, Holy Queen

Hail, holy Queen, mother of mercy, our life, our sweetness, and our hope. To thee do we cry, poor banished children of Eve. To thee do we send up our sighs mourning and weeping in this valley of tears. Turn then, most gracious advocate, thine eyes of mercy toward us, and after this our exile show us the blessed fruit of thy womb, Jesus.

O clement, O loving, O sweet Virgin Mary.

Pray for us, O Holy Mother of God.

That we may be made worthy of the promises of Christ.

The Divine Praises

Blessed be God.
Blessed be His Holy Name.
Blessed be Jesus Christ, true God and true Man.
Blessed be the Name of Jesus.
Blessed be His most Sacred Heart.
Blessed be His most Precious Blood.
Blessed be Jesus in the most Holy Sacrament of the Altar.
Blessed be the Holy Spirit, the Paraclete.
Blessed be the great Mother of God, Mary most holy.
Blessed be her holy and Immaculate Conception.
Blessed be her glorious Assumption.
Blessed be the name of Mary, Virgin and Mother.
Blessed be St. Joseph, her most chaste spouse.
Blessed be God in His angels and in His saints.

An Act of Spiritual Communion

My Jesus, I believe that You are present in the Most Holy Sacrament. I love You above all things, and I desire to receive You into my soul. Since I cannot at this moment receive You sacramentally, come at least spiritually into my heart. I embrace You as if You were already there and unite myself wholly to You. Never permit me to be separated from You. Amen.

The Morning Offering

O Jesus, through the Immaculate Heart of Mary, I offer You my prayers, works, joys, and sufferings of this day for all the intentions of Your Sacred Heart, in union with the Holy Sacrifice of the Mass throughout the world, in reparation for my sins, for the intentions of all my relatives and friends, and in particular for the intentions of the Holy Father. Amen.

Memorare

Remember, O most gracious Virgin Mary, that never was it known that anyone who fled to thy protection, implored thy help, or sought thine intercession was left unaided.

Inspired by this confidence, I fly unto thee, O Virgin of virgins, my mother; to thee do I come, before thee I stand, sinful and sorrowful. O Mother of the Word Incarnate, despise not my petitions, but in thy mercy hear and answer me. Amen.

The Anima Christi

Soul of Christ, sanctify me
Body of Christ, save me
Blood of Christ, inebriate me
Water from Christ's side, wash me
Passion of Christ, strengthen me
O good Jesus, hear me
Within Thy wounds hide me
Suffer me not to be separated from Thee
From the malicious enemy defend me
In the hour of my death call me
And bid me come unto Thee
That I may praise Thee with Thy saints
and with Thy angels
Forever and ever
Amen

The Act of Contrition

O my God, I am heartily sorry for having offended Thee, and I detest all my sins, because I dread the loss of Heaven and the pains of Hell; but most of all because they offend Thee, my God, Who art all good and deserving of all my love. I firmly resolve, with the help of Thy grace, to confess my sins, to do penance and to amend my life. Amen.

Prayer to Saint Michael the Archangel

Saint Michael the Archangel, defend us in battle. Be our defense against the wickedness and snares of the devil. May God rebuke him, we humbly pray, and do thou, O Prince of the Heavenly hosts, by the power of God, thrust into hell Satan, and all the evil spirits, who prowl about the world seeking the ruin of souls. Amen.

The Creed

I believe in God, the Father Almighty, Creator of Heaven and earth, and in Jesus Christ, His only Son, Our Lord. He was conceived by the Holy Spirit, and born of the Virgin Mary. He suffered under Pontius Pilate, was crucified, died and was buried. He descended into hell. On the third day He rose again. He ascended into Heaven, and is seated at the right hand of God the Father Almighty. He will come again to judge the living and the dead.
I believe in the Holy Spirit, the Holy Catholic Church, the communion of saints, the forgiveness of sins, the resurrection of the body, and life everlasting. Amen.

The Guardian Angel Prayer

Angel of God, my guardian dear, to whom God's love commits me here, ever this day be at my side to light and guard, to rule and guide. Amen.

The Holy Rosary

1. Make the Sign of the Cross and say, "In the name of the Father, and of the Son, and of the Holy Spirit. Amen."

2. Say the Creed.

3. Say one Our Father, three Hail Marys, and one Glory Be.

4. Announce the first Mystery (look on the next page for the Mysteries). Then pray one Our Father, ten Hail Marys, one Glory Be, and one Fátima Prayer while meditating on the Mystery.

5. Then pray one Our Father, ten Hail Marys, one Glory Be, and one Fátima Prayer for each Mystery.

6. After you have completed all the decades, say the Hail, Holy Queen.

7. Make the Sign of the Cross and say, "In the Name of the Father, and of the Son, and of the Holy Spirit. Amen."

The Mysteries of the Holy Rosary

The Joyful Mysteries (Mondays and Saturdays; Sundays during Advent and Christmas):

1. The Annunciation
2. The Visitation
3. The Nativity
4. The Presentation
5. The Finding of Jesus in the Temple

The Luminous Mysteries (Thursdays):

1. Baptism in the Jordan
2. The Wedding at Cana
3. Proclamation of the Kingdom
4. The Transfiguration
5. Institution of the Eucharist

The Sorrowful Mysteries (Tuesdays and Fridays; Sundays during Lent):

1. Agony in the Garden
2. Scourging at the Pillar
3. Crowning with Thorns
4. Carrying of the Cross
5. The Crucifixion

The Glorious Mysteries (Wednesdays and Sundays):

1. The Resurrection
2. The Ascension
3. Descent of the Holy Spirit
4. The Assumption
5. Coronation of the Blessed Virgin Mary

Quotes about the
Holy Rosary

"The Rosary is a powerful weapon to put the demons to flight
and to keep oneself from sin.... If you desire peace in your
hearts, in your homes and in your country, assemble
each evening to recite the Rosary. Let not even one day pass
without saying it, no matter how burdened you may be with
many cares and labors."
– Pope Pius XI

"How beautiful is the family that recites the Rosary every
evening." - Saint John Paul II

"Among all the devotions approved by the Church none has
been so favored by so many miracles as the devotion of the
Most Holy Rosary."
– Blessed Pius IX

"You always leave the Rosary for later, and you end up not
saying it at all because you are sleepy. If there is no other time,
say it in the street without letting anybody notice it.
It will, moreover, help you to have presence of God."
– Saint Josemaria Escriva

"The Rosary is the 'weapon' for these times."
– Saint Padre Pio

"When people love and recite the Rosary, they find it makes them better."
– Saint Anthony Mary Claret

"Say the Rosary every day to obtain world peace."
– Our Lady of Fátima

"There is no problem, I tell you, no matter how difficult it is, that we cannot solve by the prayer of the Holy Rosary."
– Sister Lúcia de Jesus Rosa dos Santos (seer of Fátima)

"If you say the Rosary faithfully until death, I do assure you that, in spite of the gravity of your sins, you shall receive a never-fading crown of glory. Even if you are on the brink of damnation… sooner or later you will be converted and will amend your life and will save your soul, if – and mark well what I say – if you say the Holy Rosary devoutly every day until death for the purpose of knowing the truth and obtaining contrition and pardon for your sins."
– Saint Louis de Montfort

"[The Rosary] is one of the greatest secrets to have come down from Heaven."
– Saint Louis de Montfort

"The Rosary can bring families through all dangers and evils."
– Servant of God Patrick Peyton

The 12 Promises of the Sacred Heart of Jesus

We can practice devotion to the Sacred Heart of Jesus by displaying His Sacred Heart prominently in our homes, having our houses Consecrated to the Sacred Heart, and by making the Nine First Fridays in honor of Jesus' Sacred Heart. The following are the promises that Jesus gave to Saint Margaret Mary Alacoque for those who are devoted to His Sacred Heart:

1. I will give them all the graces necessary in their state of life.

2. I will give peace in their families and will unite families that are divided.

3. I will console them in all their troubles.

4. I will be their refuge during life and above all in death.

5. I will bestow the blessings of Heaven on all their enterprises.

6. Sinners shall find in my Heart the source and infinite ocean of mercy.

7. Tepid souls shall become fervent.

8. Fervent souls shall rise quickly to great perfection.

9. I will bless those places wherein the image of My Heart shall be exposed and honored and will imprint My love on the hearts of those who would wear this image on their person. I will also destroy in them all disordered movements.

10. I will give to priests who are animated by a tender devotion to my Divine Heart the gift of touching the most hardened hearts.

11. Those who promote this devotion shall have their names written in my Heart, never to be effaced.

12. I promise you in the excessive mercy of my Heart that my all-powerful love will grant to all those who communicate on the First Friday in nine consecutive months, the grace of final penitence: they will not die in my disgrace, nor without receiving their Sacraments. My Divine Heart shall be their safe refuge in this last moment.

The Divine Mercy Chaplet

Step 1 – Using a Rosary, begin at the cross by making the Sign of the Cross.

(Optional Opening Prayer)
You expired, Jesus, but the source of life gushed forth for souls, and the ocean of mercy opened up for the whole world. O Fount of Life, unfathomable Divine Mercy, envelop the whole world and empty Yourself out upon us.

Step 2 - O Blood and Water, which gushed forth from the Heart of Jesus as a fountain of Mercy for us, I trust in You! (Repeat three times)

Step 3 – On the three beads of the Rosary, pray the Our Father, the Hail Mary, and the Apostles' Creed.

Step 4 – Begin each decade with the Our Father beads by praying this prayer:

Eternal Father, I offer You the Body and Blood, Soul and Divinity of Your dearly beloved Son, Our Lord Jesus Christ, in atonement for our sins and those of the whole world.

Step 5 – Complete the decade on the 10 Hail Mary beads by praying this prayer:

For the sake of His Sorrowful Passion, have mercy on us and on the whole world.

Repeat steps 4 and 5 for each decade.

Step 6 – After praying all five decades, pray the following prayer 3 times:

Holy God, Holy Mighty One, Holy Immortal One, have mercy on us and on the whole world.

Step 7 – (Optional Closing Prayer)
Eternal God, in whom mercy is endless and the treasury of compassion inexhaustible, look kindly upon us, and increase Your mercy in us, that in difficult moments, we might not despair nor become despondent, but with great confidence, submit ourselves to Your holy Will, which is Love and Mercy itself.

Amen.

The Seven Sorrows Chaplet

According to St. Bridget of Sweden's (1303-1373) visions, the Blessed Virgin promised to grant seven graces to those who meditate daily on her Sorrows:

- "I will grant peace to their families."
- "They will be enlightened about the divine Mysteries."
- "I will console them in their pains and will accompany them in their work."
- "I will give them as much as they ask for as long as it does not oppose the adorable will of my divine Son or the sanctification of their souls."
- "I will defend them in their spiritual battles with the infernal enemy, and I will protect them at every instant of their lives."
- "I will visibly help them at the moment of their death – they will see the face of their mother."
- "I have obtained this grace from my divine Son, that those who propagate this devotion to my tears and dolors will be taken directly from this earthly life to eternal happiness, since all their sins will be forgiven and my Son will be their eternal consolation and joy."

How to Pray the Seven Sorrows (Dolors) Chaplet:

Step 1 – (Optional) Make an Act of Contrition

Step 2 – Pray one Our Father and seven Hail Marys for each of Mary's Sorrows.

> **The First Sorrow:** The Prophecy of Simeon (Luke 2:25-35)
>
> **The Second Sorrow:** The Flight Into Egypt (Matthew 2:13-15)
>
> **The Third Sorrow:** The Child Jesus Lost in the Temple (Luke 2:41-50)
>
> **The Fourth Sorrow** Mary Meeting Jesus as He Carries the Cross
>
> **The Fifth Sorrow** Mary at the Foot of the Cross (John 19:25-30)
>
> **The Sixth Sorrow** Mary receives the Body of Jesus
>
> **The Seventh Sorrow:** Jesus' Burial (Luke 23:50-56)

Step 3 – Pray three Hail Marys in honor of the Blessed Mother's tears. Pray one Our Father, Hail Mary, and one Glory Be for the Holy Father's intentions. Finally, pray "Virgin Most Sorrowful, Pray for Us" three times.

Litany of Humility

By Rafael Cardinal Merry del Val (1865-1930),
Secretary of State for Pope Saint Pius X

O Jesus! meek and humble of heart, Hear me.
From the desire of being esteemed,
Deliver me, Jesus.

From the desire of being loved...
From the desire of being extolled ...
From the desire of being honored ...
From the desire of being praised ...
From the desire of being preferred to others...
From the desire of being consulted ...
From the desire of being approved ...
From the fear of being humiliated ...
From the fear of being despised...
From the fear of suffering rebukes ...
From the fear of being calumniated ...
From the fear of being forgotten ...
From the fear of being ridiculed ...
From the fear of being wronged ...
From the fear of being suspected ...

That others may be loved more than I,
Jesus, grant me the grace to desire it.

That others may be esteemed more than I ...
That, in the opinion of the world,
others may increase and I may decrease ...
That others may be chosen and I set aside ...
That others may be praised and I unnoticed ...
That others may be preferred to me in everything...
That others may become holier than I, provided that I may
become as holy as I should...

Regular Prayer Intentions

I am thankful for...

_____

_____

_____

_____

_____

_____

_____

_____

_____

Notes

_____

_____

_____

_____

_____

_____

_____

_____

_____

Books by Jennifer Harbor Rainey and Travis Rainey

A Catholic Prayer Journal for Kids

A Catholic Prayer Journal for Moms

A Catholic Prayer Journal

A Catholic Mom's Guide to Starting a Home Business

The Busy Mom's Meal Planning Journal

Catholic Planner 2019

Catholic Homeschool Planner 2019-2020
(coming spring/summer 2019)

If you join our email list, we will send you a free electronic copy of *A Catholic Prayer Journal*. Just send us an email: Webmaster@ourcatholiccorner.com. We will not send more than twelve emails each year. Thank you so much, and may God bless you!

27803173R00042

Made in the USA
San Bernardino, CA
03 March 2019